BATS

SPEAR-NOSED BATS

Pamela J. Gerholdt
ABDO & Daughters

Published by Abdo & Daughters, 4940 Viking Drive, Suite 622, Edina, Minnesota 55435.

Library bound edition distributed by Rockbottom Books, Pentagon Tower, P.O. Box 36036, Minneapolis, Minnesota 55435.

Printed in the United States.

Cover Photo credit: Paul Freed
Interior Photo credits: Paul Freed, pages 7, 9, 11, 13, 17, 19

Animals, Animals, pages 5, 21

Edited by Julie Berg

Library of Congress Cataloging-in-Publication Data

Gerholdt, Pamela J.
   Spear-nosed bat / Pamela J. Gerholdt.
     p. cm. — (Bats)
   Includes bibliographical references (p. 23) and index.
   ISBN 1-56239-502-5
1. Phyllostomus—Juvenile literature. [1. Spear-nosed bats. 2. Bats.] I. Title. II.
Series: Gerholdt, Pamela J. Bats.
QL737.C57G465   1995
599.4—dc20
                                                                95-7057
                                                                     CIP
                                                                     AC

About The Author

Pam Gerholdt has had a lifelong interest in animals. She is a member of the Minnesota Herpetological Society and is active in conservation issues. She lives in Webster, Minnesota with her husband, sons, and assorted other animals.

Contents

SPEAR-NOSED BATS

There are over 900 **species** of bats in the world. Spear-nosed bats are called "New World" bats because they are found in Central and South America. As their name suggests, spear-nosed bats have noses that look like spearheads.

All bats are **mammals**, like dogs, cats, horses, and humans. But bats do something no other mammal can do—they fly!

Spear-nosed bats are classified as members of the "New World" bat family.

WHERE THEY'RE FOUND

Bats live on all of the world's **continents** except Antarctica, the **polar regions**, and a few ocean islands. Spear-nosed bats live in many places including Brazil, Trinidad, Honduras and Paraguay.

Spear-nosed bats live in many places including Brazil, Trinidad, Honduras and Paraguay.

WHERE THEY LIVE

Spear-nosed bats live near streams, in forests, or dry open areas. They **roost** in caves, **culverts**, hollow trees, and buildings, in groups of 10 to several thousand bats.

Bats roost by hanging upside down by their feet. It's easy for them because they have 5 toes with sharp, curved claws, and knees that point backwards!

This spear-nosed bat is roosting in a tree.

SIZES

Spear-nosed bats are 3 to 5 inches (7.5 to 12.5 cm) long and weigh 1 to 3.5 ounces (28 to 98 g). They have a **wing span** of about 18 inches (45 cm).

Some bats are much bigger. Large fruit-eating bats such as flying foxes can grow to over 16 inches (40 cm) long with a wing span of over 5.5 feet (165 cm)!

Some bats are very tiny. The Kitti's hog-nosed bats grow to 1 inch (2.5 cm)—about the size of a large bumble bee! Although their bodies are small, their wing span is 6.5 inches (16.25 cm).

Spear-nosed bats are 3 to 5 inches (7.5 to 12.5 cm) long and weigh 1 to 3.5 ounces (28 to 98 g).

SHAPES

Spear-nosed bats have strong bodies and wings. Their tails are short. Their heads have small eyes and a nose that looks like a spearhead. Their ears are large with rounded tips.

Bats' wings are made of their extra long fingers and **forelimb** bones that support thin, **elastic membranes**. Two membranes, top and bottom, are sandwiched together over the bones on each wing.

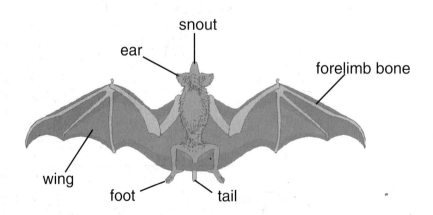

snout

ear

forelimb bone

wing

foot   tail

Spear-nosed bats have strong bodies, large head and ears, small eyes, and a spear-shaped nose.

SENSES

Spear-nosed bats have the same five senses as humans. Like over half of all bat **species**, spear-nosed bats use **echolocation** to "see" in the dark.

Most bats that use echolocation send out squeaks or clicks through the mouth. But spear-nosed bats send sound out through their nostrils, too. They use echolocation to "talk" to each other and to find food.

HOW ECHOLOCATION WORKS

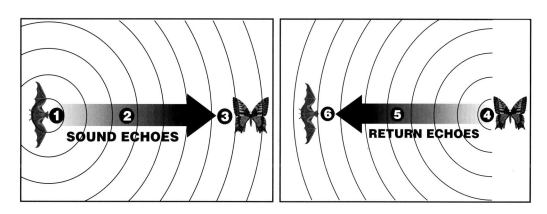

The bat sends out sound echoes (1). These echoes travel in all directions through the air (2). The sound echoes reach an object in the bat's path (3), then bounce off it (4). The return echoes travel through the air (5) and reach the bat (6). These echoes let the bat know where the object is, how large it is, and how fast it is moving.

DEFENSE

Because they are small, spear-nosed bats are "bite-sized" for many different kinds of **predators**. Cats, dogs, raccoons, and skunks eat bats. So do owls, hawks, falcons, snakes and large frogs. Large spiders eat bats that get caught in their webs. Even worse, some bats eat other bats! The bat's best defense is to fly away.

Like most bats, spear-nosed bats are **nocturnal**. This means they fly at night, avoiding many predators that hunt by day.

Bats also find safe, dark places to hide during the day when they **roost**. Spear-nosed bats' dark colors make it hard for predators to see them at night. Spear-nosed bats have a frightening appearance and fierce-looking teeth.

Spear-nosed bats have a frightening appearance when they show their fierce-looking teeth.

FOOD

A spear-nosed bat eats small **vertebrates** and insects. It uses its long tongue to catch insects.

Groups of 10 to over 100 bats leave their **roosting** sites in the evening and fly to feeding sites 1/2 to 2 miles (1 to 3.5 km) away. They are often seen feeding near gardens where bananas grow.

The spear-nosed bat uses its long tongue to catch insects.

BABIES

Spear-nosed bats **breed** once a year. They have one baby in April or May. Mother bats take good care of their babies. Female spear-nosed bats carry their new babies with them everywhere for several days. Then the babies are left at the **roost** while the mothers go out to feed themselves.

Baby spear-nosed bats can fly around the cave at about 6 weeks. They go out on their own at 2 months. Once they leave the cave, they do not return. Instead, they find other roosting sites.

Most people think bats are birds that lay eggs. But since bats are **mammals**, their babies are born live.

A group of spear-nosed bats roosting in a cave.

GLOSSARY

BREED - To produce young; also, a kind or type of animal.

CONTINENT (KAHN-tih-nent) - One of the 7 main land masses: Europe, Asia, Africa, North America, South America, Australia and Antarctica.

CULVERT - A pipe or channel which carries water under a road.

ECHOLOCATION (ek-o-lo-KAY-shun) - The use of sound waves to find objects.

ELASTIC (ee-LAS-tik) - Able to return to its normal shape after being stretched or bent.

FORELIMB - A front limb of an animal.

MAMMALS (MAM-elz) - Animals with backbones that nurse their young with milk.

MEMBRANES (MEM-branz) - Thin, easily bent layers of animal tissue.

NOCTURNAL (nok-TUR-nul) - Active by night.

POLAR - Either the Arctic (north pole) or Antarctic (south pole) regions.

PREDATOR (Pred-uh-tor) - An animal that eats other animals.

ROOST - A place, such as a cave or tree, where bats rest during the day; also, to perch.

SPECIES (SPEE-ses) - A kind or type.

VERTEBRATES (VUR-tuh-brits) - Animals with backbones.

WING SPAN - The distance from the tip of one outstretched wing to the other.

BIBLIOGRAPHY

Fenton, M. Brock. *Bats.* Facts On File, Inc., 1992.

Findley, James S. *Bats, A Community Perspective.* Cambridge University Press, 1993.

Johnson, Sylvia A. *The World Of Bats.* Lerner Publications Company, 1985.

Nowak, Ronald M. *Walker's Bats Of The World.* The Johns Hopkins University Press, 1994.

Index